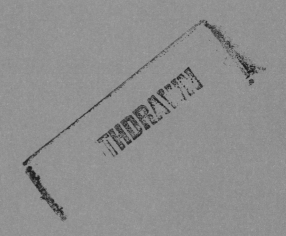

KINGFISHER READERS

level **2**

African Savanna

WITHDRAWN

Claire Llewellyn

KINGFISHER

NEW YORK

KINGFISHER
LONDON & NEW YORK

Copyright © Kingfisher 2015
Published in the United States by Kingfisher,
175 Fifth Ave., New York, NY 10010
Kingfisher is an imprint of Macmillan Children's Books, London.
All rights reserved.

Distributed in the U.S. and Canada by Macmillan,
175 Fifth Ave., New York, NY 10010

Library of Congress Cataloging-in-Publication data
has been applied for

Series editor: Thea Feldman
Literacy consultant: Ellie Costa, Bank Street School for Children, New York

ISBN 978-0-7534-7200-2 (HB)
ISBN 978-0-7534-7201-9 (PB)

Kingfisher books are available for special promotions
and premiums. For details contact: Special Markets
Department, Macmillan, 175 Fifth Ave., New York, NY 10010.

For more information please visit
www.kingfisherbooks.com

Printed in China
9 8 7 6 5 4 3 2 1
1TR/1014/WKT/UG/105MA

Picture credits
The Publisher would like to thank the following for permission to reproduce their material.
Every care has been taken to trace copyright holders. However, if there have been unintentional
omissions or failure to trace copyright holders, we apologize and will, if informed, endeavor
to make corrections in any future edition.
Top = t; Bottom = b; Center = c; Left = l; Right = r
Cover Shutterstock/Chantal de Bruijne; pages 4–5 Shutterstock/Oleg Znamenskiy; 6–7 FLPA/Bernd
Rohrschneider; 7t Shutterstock/Hedrus; 8 FLPA/Imagebroker, Rolf Schulten; 9 FLPA/Ariadne Van
Zandbergen; 10 FLPA/Bernd Rohrschneider; 11 FLPA/Frans Lanting; 12t naturepl.com/Ann & Steve Toon;
12–13 FLPA/Mitsuaki Iwago/Minden Pictures; 13t FLPA/Frans Lanting; 14 FLPA/Frans Lanting; 15 FLPA/
Frans Lanting; 16 FLPA/ Michel and Christine Denis-Huot/Biosphoto; 17t FLPA/Winfried Wisniewski;
17b Shutterstock/ajman; 18 Shutterstock/Francois Loubser; 19 FLPA/Mitsuaki Iwago/Minden Pictures;
20t FLPA/Ingo Arndt/Minden Pictures; 20b FLPA/Imagebroker; 21 FLPA/Gael Le Roch/Biosphoto; 22
Shutterstock/Francois Loubser; 23 Shutterstock/Mike Dexter; 24–25 FLPA/Shem Compion; 25t FLPA/Bernd
Rohrschneider; 26 Corbis/Martin Harvey; 27 Corbis/DLILLC; 28 FLPA/Richard Du Toit/Minden Pictures;
29t Shutterstock/Pierre-Yves BabelonPierre; 29b Corbis/ HO/Reuters; 30 naturepl.com/Suzi Eszterhas;
31t FLPA/Bernd Rohrschneider; 31b FLPA/Frans Lanting.

Contents

A grassy place

Look at this place in Africa.

It is flat and covered in grass
as far as the eye can see.

This kind of place is called
a savanna.

The savanna is sometimes warm,
and sometimes it is hot!

Two seasons

There are just two seasons
on the savanna.

One is very rainy,
and the other one is very dry.

There are only a few trees, because most trees need water all year long.

Plant-eating animals

Antelope, zebras, and many other animals that live on the savanna eat the grass.

A giraffe stretches its long neck
to reach the leaves at the top
of the trees.

An elephant family

Elephants eat grass and leaves.

They live in **herds** and look for food and water together.

All the elephants in a herd are
related to each other.

There can be 100 elephants
in one herd!

Meat-eating animals

Some savanna animals
hunt and eat other animals.

Scorpions eat mice and insects.

Lions hunt bigger animals.

Animals that hunt and eat other animals are called **predators**.

Nowhere to hide

It is easy for a predator to see **prey** animals on the savanna.

Many prey animals live in herds, and watch out for predators together.

When they see a predator coming,
prey animals run as fast as they can!

Leftovers!

Some meat eaters, such as jackals, do not hunt.

They eat the leftover meat that lions leave behind.

Animals that eat leftover meat
are called **scavengers**.

Scavenger birds,
such as vultures,
use their strong
beaks to rip into
a **carcass**.

Savanna birds

Many birds live on the savanna.

This weaverbird used its beak to weave a ball-shaped nest out of grass!

The ostrich is the biggest bird.
It is taller than the tallest person!

Ostriches can't fly, so they walk
or run everywhere they go.

Keeping cool

How do some savanna animals stay cool? They build homes using soil!

termites

termite mound

Aadvarks dig deep burrows
in the soil to stay cool.

Termites build nests inside
giant mounds of soil,
where it is cool and airy.

The dry season

During the dry season
on the savanna,
rivers and waterholes dry up,
and the grass dies.

Each year, some animals **migrate** more than 1,000 miles (1,600 kilometers) to find food and water.

The great migration

The yearly wildebeest migration is an amazing thing to see!

When the dry season starts, more than one million wildebeest migrate together, looking for food and water.

They return home when the rainy
season starts, and the grass begins
to grow.

Savanna people

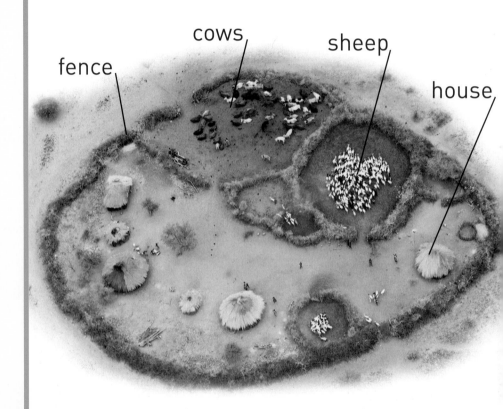

fence

cows

sheep

house

Some people live in villages on the savanna.

Many of them raise cows, goats, and sheep.

People get meat and milk
from their animals.

Each village has a thick fence
to keep out predators.

Animals in danger

Savanna animals face many dangers.
Many are losing their land to farms.

Thousands of animals are shot each
year by farmers or **poachers**.

Poachers kill rhinos and elephants,
to sell their horns and tusks.

If the killing doesn't stop,
these animals could become **extinct**.

Protecting animals

There are national parks on savanna where animals are protected.

People cannot take their land, and **rangers** protect the animals from poachers.

Every year people visit the parks
to see the animals where they live.

They are on **safari**!

Safaris bring money
to local people
and help keep
animals safe.

Glossary

carcass the body of a dead animal

extinct when all of one kind of animal has died

herds large groups of the same kind of animal

migrate to move from one place to another for part of the year

poachers people who shoot animals against the law

predator an animal that hunts and eats other animals

prey an animal that is hunted and eaten by other animals

rangers people in charge of protecting animals and parks

safari a trip to see wild animals in Africa

scavengers animals that eat the bodies of dead animals they find